EXPLORE
LAKELAND
BY CAR

Describing more than 50 places
to visit in all parts of Lakeland

DALESMAN

DALESMAN PUBLISHING COMPANY LTD.,
CLAPHAM, VIA LANCASTER, LA2 8EB

First published 1972
Eighth edition 1989
Reprinted 1992
© Dalesman Publishing Co. Ltd., 1989

ISBN: 1 85568 043 2

Printed by Peter Fretwell & Sons Ltd.,
Goulbourne Street, Keighley, West Yorkshire BD21 1PZ

Contents

Maps by E. Gower.

Introduction

"EXPLORE", says the dictionary, means "to inquire into". The first word of the title of this book is of greater significance, for it is the motorist who wishes to inquire rather than be directed who will derive most from this work.

It does not consist of the usual series of motor runs with all their tedious "turn lefts" and "bear rights", but instead details some of the outstanding facets of the Lake District which can readily be seen by car. These range from tracts of outstanding country to interesting settlements, and from ancient monuments to country houses open to the public.

The general map will help motorists to select their itineraries, while the sectional maps and the italicised directions should also be of assistance. Suggestions for short walks are intended as an antidote to car weariness.

Lakeland is popularly associated with the "classic" central region of Cumbria (since April, 1974, the name for a new administrative area). The sections which cover the central area of high fells and lakes are Windermere and Coniston (D), Ambleside and the Langdales (E), Borrowdale and Buttermere (H), Keswick and Northern Lakeland (G), and Penrith and Ullswater (F).

Windermere and Coniston includes not only two of the best-known lakes in England, but also such delightful villages as Hawkshead and Sawrey as well as the extensive Grizedale Forest. Ambleside and the Langdales takes in the smaller lakes of Grasmere and Rydal Water, the twin valleys of Great and Little Langdale and the ever-impressive Grasmere village.

Borrowdale and Buttermere describes the many points of interest to be seen on the famous circular drive past Derwentwater and over Honister Pass, while the lakes of Bassenthwaite and Thirlmere and the communities of Calderbeck and Cockermouth feature in Keswick and Northern Lakeland. The section on Penrith and Ullswater covers the north-east corner of Lakeland.

The popularity of the central region of the Lake District has tended to relegate to undeserved obscurity much of the very fine country on its fringes. The motorist will find it more than worthwhile to explore the periphery of Lakeland, particularly at weekends and peak holiday periods when the heart of the National Park can get very congested.

Opposite: Spirit of Lakeland. Autumn on Grasmere, with Helm Crag in the distance. *(Tom Parker)*

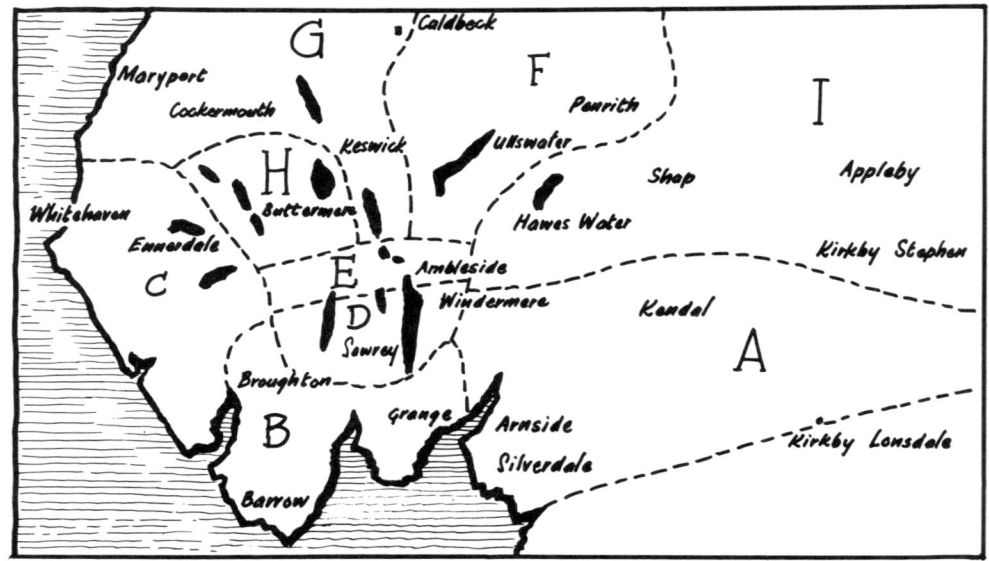

Kendal and the South-East (A) sounds an unpromising area, but away from the roar of rushing traffic are some fine country houses and many sylvan tracts of rural beauty.

Turning northwards from Furness brings the visitor to Western Lakeland (C), a region which would be far more popular if it were not so inaccessible. Here are the superb lakes of Wastwater and Ennerdale Water, and a long stretch of coastline open to the breakers of the Irish Sea.

Away on the opposite side of Cumbria is Eastern Lakeland (I). This is where the Shap Fells taper away to the broad Eden Valley, which in turn gives way to the Cross Fell range and the backbone of the Pennines. Once again, there are many surprises for the motorist who is willing to explore.

A.

Kendal and the South-East

THE south-east corner of Lakeland is seen by hundreds of thousands of motorists but known by comparatively few. For it forms the gateway to the Lake District National Park, through which drivers normally rush headlong towards the scenic splendours beyond. Yet those willing to pause and explore will find that this is a region of surprising interest and scenic charm.

Kendal's environs soon give way to pleasing countryside. To the east is an area of undulating hills separating the Kent and Lune valleys. Beyond this Middleton Fell and the unmistakable Howgills form the boundary with Yorkshire. To the west the ground rises and then falls towards the Lyth Valley, while to the south is the peninsula of Arnside and Silverdale — encompassing great variety in a small area.

KENDAL

(Can hardly be missed; now by-passed by Lakeland-bound traffic)

This large town is a happy blend of ancient and modern. Shops of the most contemporary design stand cheek by jowl with venerable-looking archways — the entrance to yards which formed a source of refuge in the days of the Scots raids. The town lines the bank of the river Kent, where the normally placid waters contrast sharply with bustling Stricklandgate and Finkle Street.

Its most historic landmark is the castle, built by Ivo de Talebois about 1805. It was the birthplace and home of Katherine Parr whose father, Sir Thomas, was controller of the king's household and died when she was only five. Katherine became the sixth wife of Henry VIII in 1543. The castle was given to the Parr family in the 12th century and remained in their possession until the 17th when it was allowed to fall into ruins. The public has free access to the remains.

A present day mecca for visitors is Abbot Hall, at the south end of the town just off the A6. It was built in 1759 as a private house, probably by John Carr, and in June 1962 was opened as an art gallery by Princess Margaret. Many fine examples of Chippendale, Sheraton and Hepplewhite furniture are to be seen on the ground floor which has been restored to its 18th century grandeur. The first floor has been converted into four galleries for housing art exhibitions. Royalty returned to Kendal in 1971 when Princess Alexandra opened the Museum of Lakeland Life and Industry, adapted

Abbot Hall, Kendal, opened as an art gallery by Princess Margaret in 1962. The former stable block is now the Museum of Lakeland Life and Industry.

from the former stable block at Abbot Hall. This has been laid out on the latest lines and is in many ways pioneering the art of display.

Other features of Kendal well worth a visit are the parish church (the largest in England), the Brewery Arts Centre in Highgate, the Museum in Station Road and the Castle Dairy in Wildman Street.

ARNSIDE AND SILVERDALE

(Twin villages to the west of the A6 north of Carnforth)

Morecambe Bay sprouts two finger-like estuaries — the Leven and the Kent. Butting into the Kent like a clenched fist is a peninsula sporting coppice woods, a network of minor roads and a series of small villages. The two best known of these villages are Arnside and Silverdale.

Arnside overlooks the estuary and the 50 piers of the long viaduct which carries the former Furness Railway from Carnforth to Barrow. The village was only a tiny hamlet at the end of the 18th century, its expansion stemming from the arrival of the railway in 1857. The promenade and embankment were made about 1897.

Arnside is dominated by the 522 feet high Knott, a rocky outcrop on which the first human settlement in the district would be made. Largely owned by the National Trust, it provides a first-rate vantage point and has on its summit a useful mountain indicator. There are many other well-signposted walks in the vicinity, the most invigorating being along the edge of the estuary.

So much silting up has taken place that it is quite safe to walk along the

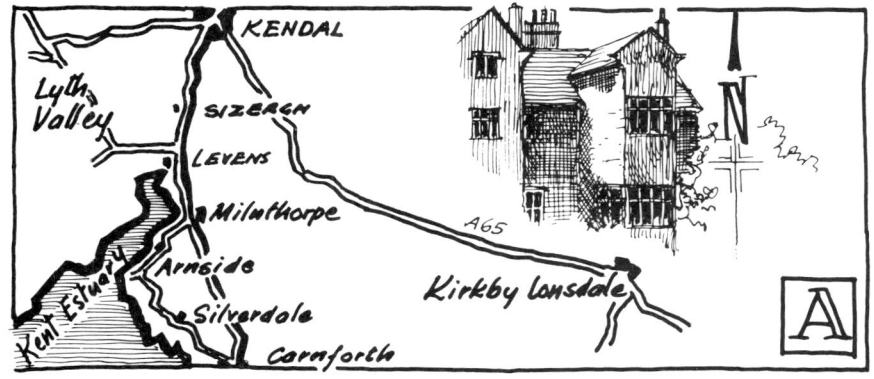

shore from Arnside to Silverdale at low tide. Silverdale is sited a little inland, but the shore can be approached at a number of points. The local walks are again most adequately signposted.

A popular walk ends at Jenny Brown's Point. The marshes are close at hand, while an isolated chimney is the remains of an 18th-century copper-smelting works. Little is known about Jenny Brown, except that she was an old lady who lived at the large house on the shore about 250 years ago and kept pigs.

LEVENS HALL

(At the point where the A590 Barrow road leaves the A6)

The first Levens Hall was built in the 12th century, the remains of its pele tower forming the oldest portion of the present building. The original structure is thought to be the work of Mathew de Redman, a member of a family which had strong connections with Lancashire and Westmorland.

De Redman's descendants owned Levens Hall until 1652 when it was sold to Sir Alan Bellingham. Many alterations and additions to the property were made by his son James who inserted much fine plaster work and panelling. The last Bellingham sold the building to Colonel James Graham in 1688, since when it has always passed by marriage or descent, culminating in the present ownership by Mr. Robin Bagot.

The visitor to the hall will be impressed by the remarkable collections of valuable paintings, silver and furniture, including many by Gillow of Lancaster. The gardens are equally impressive and are particularly noted for their topiary work. This is the creation of Monsieur Beaumont who came to England from Versailles to lay out gardens for King James II and was later employed by Colonel Graham. One tree, the Great Umbrella, is over 800 years old.

The former brew house in the grounds has been adapted to house a

9

fascinating Steam Collection — the only display in Britain of stationary engines regularly running under steam. Engines spaced out round the walls have a history as varied as their shapes.

On the opposite side of the A6 is Levens Park, a classic example of late 17th-century landscaping.

SIZERGH CASTLE

(Just off the A6, three miles south of Kendal)

Once described as "one of the noblest homes in all England", Sizergh Castle has been occupied by members of the Strickland family since 1239. They inherited the lands on which it stands from Gervase Deincourt, to whom they had been granted by Henry II. The Strickland family has played a prominent part in the history of England, fighting at Hastings and during the Wars of the Roses, as well as at the battles of Agincourt and Edgehill.

The unusual name of the castle is of Scandinavian derivation and was originally "Sigaritherge", meaning Sigarth's dairy farm. It is now a National Trust property, and is open to the public on Wednesdays between April and September. The gardens are also open on Tuesdays and Thursdays.

The centre of the building is the ancient pele tower, around which is built the hall and the Elizabethan wings. The contents include fine Tudor panelling, exquisite Flemish tapestry of the 17th century and many lovely portraits. Some magnificent inlaid panelling from a room known as the Inlaid Chamber was unfortunately sold in 1890 and is now in the Victoria and Albert Museum. But the room still has its original stucco ceiling and frieze formed of rib pattern and floral motif.

Katherine Parr also figures in the story of Sizergh, for there is a tradition that she slept in a splendid bedroom hung with tapestry. A tablecloth and a counterpane of white satin, embroidered with pictures of flowers and gorgeous birds and butterflies are said to have been worked by her.

SIZERGH CASTLE

10

B.   Cartmel and Furness

THE ancient and extensive parish of Cartmel must not be confused with either the village of Cartmel or the hamlet of Cartmel Fell. It has a perimeter of some forty miles, and except for two miles this is made up entirely of water. To the east the boundary is the river Winster, and to the west the river Leven and the eastern edge of Windermere. In the south the curving shore of Morecambe Bay forms a natural frontier, while in the north the only section of the border on dry land extends from Storr to Winster.

It was not until the coming of the railway in 1857 that the district was firmly linked with the outside world. Today Cartmel is a favourite holiday area. It has a genial climate, a pleasing blend of coastal and inland scenery, an unusually large number of narrow lanes and paths among sylvan surroundings, and a heritage that is rich in ancient buildings. It is close to central Lakeland but not so close as to be overcrowded.

The equally ancient parish of Furness was formerly even more isolated for the Leven estuary formed an additional obstacle to communication. Its inland boundaries are the Duddon, the Brathay, Windermere and the Leven, and also includes Walney Island and the smaller islands of Piel, Foulney and Roa (the last two are now tethered to the mainland by means of causeways).

CARTMEL PRIORY

(Follow unclassified but well-signposted roads for two miles from Grange-over-Sands)

The delightful village of Cartmel is so overshadowed by the priory as to be termed "a cathedral city in miniature". It was founded in 1188 by the black-habited canons regular of St. Augustine through the generosity of William Mareshall, Baron of Cartmel and Earl of Pembroke. He directed that the priory should "never be raised to the dignity of an abbey", and by the time of the Dissolution it was only a small community with ten real canons and about fifty brethren in all.

Cartmel priory was the only monastic church in Lancashire which escaped destruction at the Dissolution; moreover it was roofless for only eight years. In the period 1610-23, George Preston of Holker Hall carried out a full restoration, an inscription stating that he "repaired this Church, being in great decay, with a new roof of timber, and beautified it very decently with pretty plaister work, adorned the chancel with curiously-carved woodwork, and placed therein a pair of organs of great value".

When studying the exterior of the priory it is important to remember that the building still has genuine monastic walls. The most striking feature is the

11

1410 belfry tower which is built diagonally on top of the original lantern tower. This freak piece of building — thought to be unique in the world — has horrified at least one famous architect who, describing it as "somewhat audacious", was unable to see any reason why the structure had not collapsed long ago.

The interior of the priory shows the architecture of the transitional period between Norman and Early English. Riveting the attention is the choir with its 26 stalls dating from 1450. On the underside of the seats are misericords depicting a wide variety of subjects including a cock, an eagle, a dragon, a pelican and a greyhound.

GRANGE-OVER-SANDS

(Turn off the A590 Barrow road at Lindale and follow B5277 for two miles.)

Grange has acquired an enviable reputation as a place where ailments such as arthritis and rheumatism are cured almost instantly, and where bank

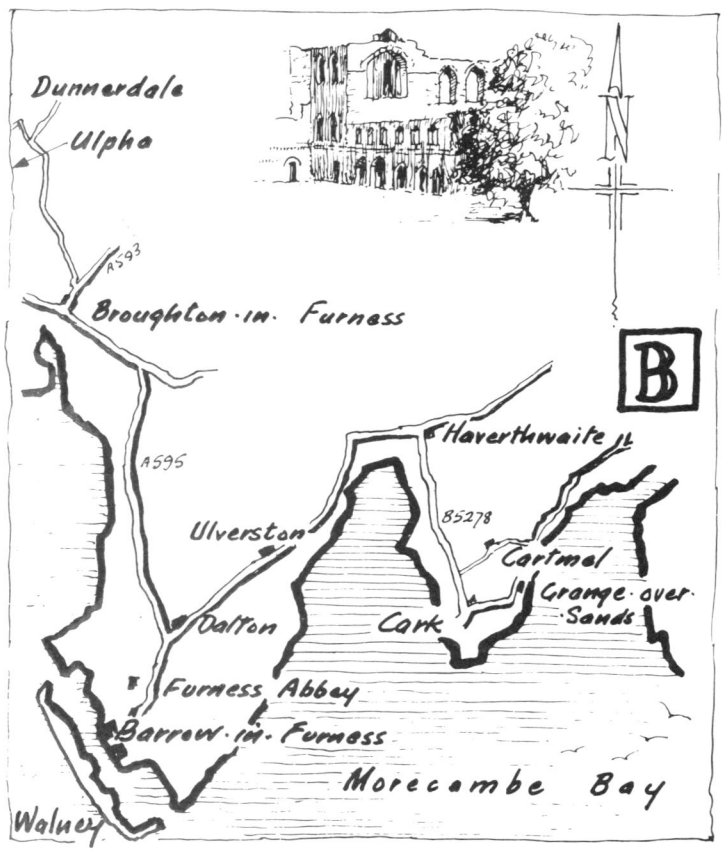

Attractive corner of Cartmel, a village sometimes termed "a cathedral city in miniature" because of its massive and magnificent priory church. *(F. Leonard Jackson)*

managers seek retirement to live merrily into their nineties. Geography is largely responsible for these health-giving properties. Grange faces south over Morecambe Bay and is wafted by warm sea breezes as well as warm air currents carried north by the influence of the Gulf Stream. On the landward side Hampsfell forms the perfect windbreak. Snow rarely settles on the ground, while the springtime temperatures are reputed to be the highest in northern England.

Until the middle of the last century Grange consisted of just a few whitewashed fishermen's cottages. It was "discovered", and acquired the suffix "-over-Sands", with the opening of the railway in 1857.

A walk along the promenade can be a most rewarding experience. Morecambe Bay's sandy expanse is thronged with birds at certain seasons of the year, notably during times of migration. Residents include colourful Shelduck, curlews, sharp-eyed redshanks, herons and black-headed gulls. In spring come the fleeting hosts of migrants such as knot, dunlin, turnstone and godwit.

Of all the viewpoints around Grange there is nothing to equal Hampsfell Hospice, a pilgrimage to the top of this limestone plateau being an essential part of a visit to the area. The most direct approach is to follow Hampsfell Road past Yewbarrow Lodge and up a steep hill to a field gate; here turn sharp to the right alongside a wall, pass through another gate and then bear left up the brow to reach the hospice at a point 727 feet above sea level.

The views from the hospice range over scores of Lakeland and Pennine mountains, and in exceptionally clear conditions can extend to Snowdon and the Isle of Man.

HOLKER HALL

(Alongside the B5277 Grange-Haverthwaite road just north of Cark village.)

Holker Hall, seat of the Cavendishes for over 200 years, is one of the relatively few stately homes in the north-west open to the public. The hall was erected at the end of the 16th century by George Preston on land belonging to Cartmel Priory; the close connection between the two best-known buildings in this district has always been maintained.

The estate passed by marriage to Sir William Lowther who demolished the original hall and rebuilt "in a more elegant style". Additions were made by Lord George Cavendish in the late 18th century, but in 1840 the house was entirely rebuilt in a style closely resembling the original building by the Earl of Burlington — later to become the 7th Duke of Devonshire. He stated, "Chatsworth is my palace but Holker is my home".

In 1871 came a set-back when the west wing with all its valuable books, pictures and furniture was entirely destroyed by fire. The subsequent reconstruction gave Holker a solid, Victorian look, but the hall is nevertheless a pleasing amalgam of architectural styles. There are many interesting exhibitions including the superb Lakeland Motor Museum and special events at weekends — a good day out for the entire family!

Holker's gardens are sheltered from the cold winds, and contain many trees and shrubs rarely found in the north. Early scarlet rhododendrons in February give way to camelias, magnolias and flowering cherries, which in turn are followed by roses, lilies, hydrangeas and heathers. A herd of fallow deer in the park is one of the largest and oldest established in the country.

FURNESS ABBEY

(On a minor road just off the A590 at the approaches to Barrow, 1½ miles after passing through Dalton)

The Furness Abbey story starts in 1124 when a small monastic house was erected on the north of the river Ribble near Tulketh by Stephen, later king of England. It was given to the Carthusian Order, whose members soon decided that a site should be sought for a larger monastery. They eventually came to Furness and selected a position in a most beautiful wooded valley known as Bekansgill — the Vale of the Deadly Nightshade.

Furness Abbey became second only to Fountains as the richest Cistercian house in England, but ultimately its power began to corrupt. It seems that at one stage the abbot had two wives, and one of the monks no less than five!

Today, more than 400 years after the dissolution of the monasteries, the abbey's ruins remain an impressive sight. The soft red sandstone blends attractively with the surrounding woodland, and the visitor to the site will find it difficult to believe that he is on the outskirts of a large industrial town.

Perhaps the most impressive remains are those of the church which was about 275 feet long and had walls over five feet thick. Also still standing are parts of the dormitories, cloisters and refectory. A small museum has been established in the 14th century infirmary chapel.

THE DUDDON VALLEY

(Scenically, it is best to drive up the valley rather than down it. Turn right at Duddon Bridge, one mile west of Broughton-in-Furness on the A595)

The River Duddon was immortalised by Wordsworth, who managed to make it the subject of no less than 34 of his sonnets. It runs through a narrow valley which is well-wooded for much of its length but in its upper reaches becomes increasingly wild. Although it does not contain a lake, the Duddon valley — or Dunnerdale — encompasses almost every other type of scenery to be found in the area.

From Duddon Bridge to Ulpha there is a road on either side of the valley, but that on the east is the easiest and most direct. It climbs quickly and steeply until it is over 200 feet above the river, and then descends gradually along the side of Dunnerdale Fell.

Ulpha, a small hamlet, is the junction for a road that climbs steeply on to Birker Fell and runs over to Eskdale. It passes close to Devoke Water, a lake three-quarters of a mile long but little known because it is away from main roads. Just over a mile further up the valley is Hall Dunnerdale, from where a road goes over the slopes of Stickle Pike to Broughton Mills.

The final settlement in the valley is Seathwaite, near where the Duddon flows through a spectacular gorge between Low Crag and Holling House Tongue. This is also the point at which energetic motorists can follow the Walna Scar track — it provides fine walking as it climbs to a summit of almost 2,000 feet. Around the head of the valley is a new Spruce forest.

There are two ways out of the head of the Duddon valley — both of them spectacular. Westbound motorists can enter Eskdale via Hard Knott Pass, which provides perhaps the most Alpine-like motoring in this country. Less demanding but still exhilerating is the eastbound exit over Wrynose Pass to Little Langdale.

C.   Western Lakeland

THE western edge of Lakeland is now very much a region for the day visitor. Recent improvements to the A590 and A595 through Newby Bridge, Greenodd and Broughton-in-Furness have greatly shortened the journey from the south. This is also a scenic route, especially if the Corney Fell road is taken from Duddon Bridge to a point just south of Ravenglass. This saves several miles and from its 1,300ft summit offers a splendid panorama across the Irish Sea towards the Isle of Man. From the north the most attractive and generally the quickest route is via Ennerdale Bridge and the "Cold Fell road" to Calderbridge.

Western Lakeland has a character and charm all of its own. It is here that the fells nudge down to the Cumberland coast, making it possible to exchange sandy beaches for the windy mountain heights within little more than an hour. From the Duddon estuary to St. Bees Head there is a virtually unbroken stretch of uncrowded beaches, offering fine panoramic seascapes.

Inland are the lakes of Ennerdale Water and Wastwater, magnificent in their grandeur and, because of their position, less thronged than their more eastern counterparts. Rivers include the Calder, the Ehen (not to be confused with the Eden), and three which flow into a common estuary at Ravenglass — the Esk, Irt and Mite.

There are some impressive mountain summits north of Wasdale, but perhaps the most conspicuous upland mass is the isolated peak of Black Combe. With a summit level of 1,970 feet this just fails to achieve mountain status, but because of its proximity to the coast offers superb views to the north and south.

THE RAVENGLASS & ESKDALE RAILWAY

(Extends from Ravenglass to Dalegarth. Most passengers will join at Ravenglass, which lies just off the A595 6½ miles north of Bootle.)

Since it was opened in 1875 the Ravenglass and Eskdale Railway has twice had the threat of abandonment hanging over its head. Today it is supported by a preservation society, and is again thriving. Some 200,000 people a year enjoy the thrill of a journey from the shore of the Irish Sea to the foot of Scafell behind a miniature steam locomotive.

Always known locally as "Ratty", the railway was initially built as a 3ft. gauge line to tap iron ore deposits in the valley. The mineral workings soon failed, but the line managed to struggle on by catering for the tourists which even then were flocking to Lakeland in considerable numbers. The railway closed in 1912, but was taken over by Mr. W. J. Bassett-Lowke, the famous model-maker, and relaid to a gauge of 15 inches. The work was completed by 1917, and additional prosperity came in 1922 with the opening of a granite quarry alongside the line.

By the 1950s "Ratty" was in trouble again. Increasing competition had made the quarry uneconomical and in 1953 it closed. Once more it was found that the line could not survive on passenger traffic alone, and in September 1960 it was offered for sale by auction. Over the years scores of people had come to love the little railway, and were not prepared to see it go without a struggle. The Ravenglass and Eskdale Railway Preservation Society was formed and subscriptions and donations started to pour in. At the auction held at Gosforth Village Hall a successful bid of £12,000 cheated the scrap merchants. Today "Ratty" is more healthy than ever before, but still needs all the help it can get.

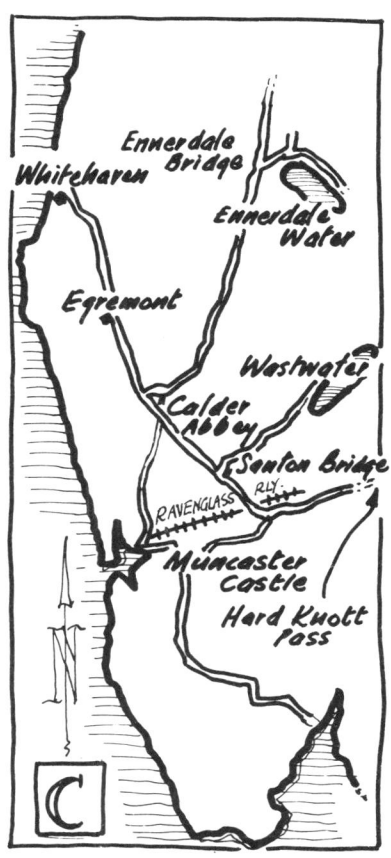

There can be few more memorable holiday experiences than travelling behind a miniature steam engine through one of the finest of Lakeland's valleys.

MUNCASTER CASTLE

(Alongside the A595, six miles north of Bootle)

Muncaster Castle, from a strictly commercial standpoint, is a stately home which suffers from its remoteness from large centres of population. It deserves to be much better known, both for its contents and its gardens.

The castle is the home of Sir William Pennington-Ramsden, and has belonged to the Pennington family since the 13th century. In 1325 the pele tower was erected: it is tunnel-vaulted at ground level and has a spiral stairway. Further enlargements were carried out in the 15th century, but most of the building which is seen today is the work of Anthony Salvin and was built for the fourth Lord Muncaster between 1862 and 1866.

A fascinating legend concerns the Luck of Muncaster, said to be a gift of Henry VI who stayed for a brief spell with the Penningtons. The room in which the monarch slept is still preserved with great care, and the carved oak bedstead on which he rested bears his initials and a crown.

HARD KNOTT

(The most difficult road in Lakeland, linking Eskdale with Dunnerdale)

Hard Knott Pass is not for the timorous. It follows the course of the old Roman road from Ravenglass to Ambleside, and at the Eskdale side climbs a thousand feet in little over a mile.

A feature of outstanding archaeological interest is Hardknott Castle, the best-preserved Roman fort in Cumberland south of Hadrian's Wall. The Ministry of Works acquired the site in the 1950s; it consists of a small three-acre stone auxiliary fort, an external bath house and a parade ground lying near the road.

Most visitors to Hardnott have been impressed by the site and its setting. R. S. Ferguson, writing in 1892, called it "an enchanting fortress in the air". Hugh Walpole in *Katherine Christian* refers to "a fortress . . . so strong that the skeleton of it would last forever, so beautiful because all around it are some of the greatest mountains of Cumberland, built by the Romans — the only power that subdued the savage north".

WASTWATER

(Turn off the A595 at either Holmrook or Gosforth and follow well-signposted unclassified roads)

Wastwater is perhaps the most awe-inspiring of all the English lakes. It is hemmed in by the great mountains of Red Pike (2,269 ft.), Kirk Fell (2,630 ft.), Great Gable (2,949 ft.) and Scafell Pike (3,210 ft.). Its waters can look

Wastwater, with at its head the brooding 2,949ft peak of Great Gable.

decidedly ominous for this is also the deepest of the English lakes. It takes the form of a fissure which plunges beneath the surface of the water for more than 250 feet — the bottom of the lake is below sea level.

Adding an extra element of grandeur are the famous screes on the south-east side of Wastwater. These extend the whole length of the lake and have been formed by gradual erosion. They are "streaked with brilliant hues of red and brown, like the changing colours of a pigeon's neck".

Wastwater and Wasdale have been described as "as grand a combination as can be found in the British Isles". It was an American who said to Nancy Price "that it was the last place God made, and He has lost His touch". Nancy herself said, "Imagine a black mass of rock hollowed out by a great cheese scoop into the shape of a cradle; that was something like the effect the mountains and dales have to me."

D.

Windermere and Coniston

WINDERMERE, England's largest lake, lies in silurian country, a little to the south of the volcanic rocks that give grandeur to points north of Ambleside. Windermere is most attractive — 10½ miles of relatively narrow lake, with promontories and islets set in a countryside of low wooded hills.

Windermere is the most popular of the Cumbrian lakes, and on a sunny day in August there can be over 2,000 boats on the water. The local authority owns 900 moorings and has 120 rock and fairway markers; there is actually a speed limit, which means that sections of Windermere have a "highway" status.

Steamers, each named after a bird, operate between Lakeside and Waterhead. A ferryboat, the *Drake*, maintained by the county council, plies between Ferry Nab and near *Ferry Hotel*.

Visit, just to the north of Bowness, a remarkable Steamboat Museum; the major exhibits are seen afloat under a capacious roof.

The smaller Coniston Water is bounded in the west by the rising ground on which part of the large Grizedale Forest was planted.

BOWNESS AND WINDERMERE TOWN

(Mid-way, to the east, of Windermere Lake)

Bowness is the oldest village of the two. Its parish has the land "below the beck", the old name being Undermillbeck. Windermere town developed, with the coming of the railway, from a number of hamlets lying up the hillside from the lake. One of those settlements was Applethwaite; it is here that St. Mary's church stands.

A tourist at Bowness will be entranced by the colour and activity around Bowness Bay, where there are facilities for hiring boats and fishing tackle. Bowness church evokes a spirit of long ago with its outstanding east window — filled with stained glass brought from Cartmel Priory and of 14th century date — plus many ancient mural inscriptions.

Near Bowness is the National Trust-owned Queen Adelaide's Hill. Three enjoyable approaches to the Hill are on Rayrig Road (from Bowness), Birthwaite Road and a footpath near St. Mary's church (from Windermere). Public seats have been set out, and the lakeshore includes a portion fenced off as a swimming space which the visiting public can use.

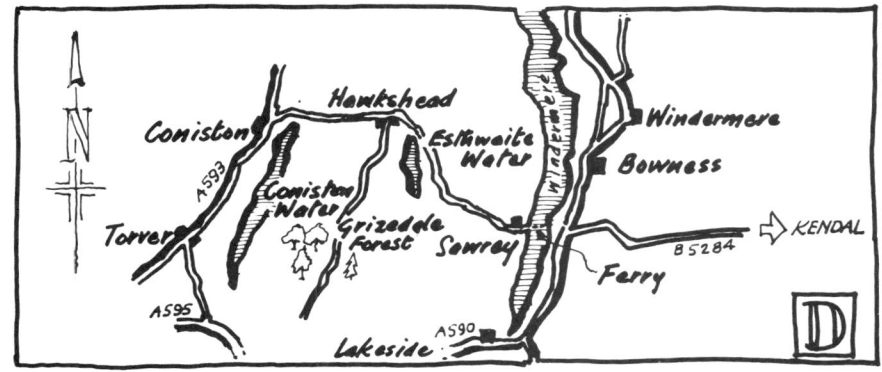

On Orrest Head, approached from almost opposite the station entrance, is a mountain indicator. The height above sea level is only 783 feet, but there are uninterrupted views of Windermere lake and the Cumbrian mountains.

NEWBY BRIDGE AND LAKESIDE

(At the outflow of Windermere, and close to the A590 between Lindale and Greenodd)

The river surging under Newby Bridge is the Leven, outflow of Windermere, heading for Morecambe Bay, which it joins near Ulverston.

Fell Foot, on the east shore of the lake (and immediately opposite Lakeside) is a County Park of the National Trust. About 18 acres are open to the public.

From Newby Bridge, a road leads to the west of Windermere lake, with Hawkshead as the destination. Lakeside, beside this road, is the terminus for the white-hulled lake vessels. Here, too, is the end of a branch railway which has been reopened to passengers from Haverthwaite. A preservation society keeps the railway spirit alive, and old rolling stock has been assembled.

The main season for modern Windermere cruising begins in May, but traditionally a cruise takes place at Easter. The four boats — *Swan, Teal, Swift* and *Tern* — are "steamers" only in the traditional sense. Coal, boilers and funnels long since gave way to engines fuelled by diesel oil. The service is being steadily improved. There are bars on the vessels, which break the journey to Waterhead by calling at Bowness Bay.

BROCKHOLE NATIONAL PARK CENTRE

(Just off the A591, between Windermere and Ambleside)

Brockhole, the Lake District National Park Centre, attracts tens of thousands of visitors each season, most of whom have crisp memories of the Englishness of its style, its setting with gardens giving way to lawns, and views to the rocky lake shore. There are walks shaded by lofty trees.

21

Classic panorama of Windermere, with in the distance the Crinkles, Bowfell and the Langdale Pikes. *(Tom Parker)*

Cars are driven into a park with space for 300 vehicles. Covered with mono-blocks, much of the parking area is, in effect, a hard grass surface rather than giving the impression — as do many parks — of being a bleak section of the high Cairngorms.

In the house the Gaddums built are exciting exhibitions telling the story of the Lake District from the earliest times to the daily life of the present day. There is a café in which 100 people can be comfortably seated under a roof that is timber-lined, topped off with local slate.

Visitors may arrive by water, in boats from Bowness that call at the jetty; they stride along a path between trees to open ground (part of the 32 acre estate) and see the old home of the Gaddums, white, elegant, above terraces where, in spring, azaleas and rhododendrons bloom.

The whole of the ground floor of Brockhole is devoted to the main exhibition, telling the Lakeland story in models, pictures and with full use of audio-visual aids. There are twice weekly guided tours of the gardens from May to September.

There, too, is a Poet's Corner, set in an alcove, with a broad window leading the eye across the Brockhole estate to the lake and, beyond, to the turreted hills of Langdale. Voices recorded on tape give readings from writers associated with the area, including William Wordsworth, Arthur Ransome and Beatrix Potter. The World of Beatrix Potter Exhibition recreates the tales of this immortal children's writer.

The farmer, so often overlooked by those writing about Lakeland is seen as the man who sustains the basic industry, agriculture. One section of the main exhibition relates to the construction and maintenance of drystone walls.

In the lecture theatre, films and slide sequences on various aspects of the Lake District are shown throughout the day. In addition, throughout each season there is a daily list of special events: day courses, film shows, "Meet the Author" sessions, and events for children such as "Young Explorers" and "Young Birdwatchers" which make use of the Centre's grounds and wooded lake-shore. Teddy Bear's Picnics are arranged in the summer.

THE SAWREYS

(Beside the road from Ferry House, by Windermere to Hawkshead)

Near and Far Sawrey are named after their positions in relation to Hawkshead. Near them is Esthwaite Water, which is one-and-a-half miles long and about one-third of a mile broad, having a maximum depth of 80 feet.

What marks out Near Sawrey from other local villages is Hill Top, a house owned by Beatrix Potter. She left it to the National Trust, and it is open to the public at prescribed times. Hill Top contains much material connected with the writer of the famous children's books.

For a time Hill Top was Beatrix Potter's home. Later, the house was simply her workplace, for she married her solicitor, William Heelis, and they went to live at Castle Cottage.

Hill Top was one small property in a 4,000-acre estate which Miss Potter built up and presented to the National Trust. She died in 1943, aged 77. Within three years the place — virtually untouched since the days she visited it — was "open to view".

Anyone who compares the paintings reproduced in her books with the scenes today will be impressed by the lack of change. Even the nesting place of Jemima Puddleduck in a rhubarb patch in the garden is unspoilt!

HAWKSHEAD

(At a meeting place of roads from Ambleside, Coniston, the Ferry and Newby Bridge)

Quaint, an overworked word, can be readily applied to Hawkshead, which is a place of white-walled buildings, squares, alleys, winding roads and flagged footpaths.

The name of the village is derived from the Norse period, and the church

— dedicated to St. Michael of All Angels — stands on the knoll where the original Norse settlement was established. Hawkshead parish stretches from Brathay, near Ambleside, to Graythwaite, and from the shores of Windermere at Low Wray to Tarn Hows. A large car park was made to cater for the increasing number of day visitors.

Wordsworth went to school at Hawkshead. The old Grammar School, founded by Archbishop Sandys in the 16th century, was last used as a school in 1909. Now it is governed by a Foundation, and can be visited. The classroom is large and full of interest. On the walls are several portraits of Wordsworth, who was a pupil here for eight years from 1778. Visitors look into a glass-topped case at a ledger kept by Anne Tyson, Wordsworth's landlady.

Tarn Hows, to which one can motor from Hawkshead Hill, a point mid-way between Hawkshead and Coniston (look out for the road signs), is frequently cited as an example of all that is scenically of the best on Lakeland. The area is attractive but the valley was dammed to make the tarns. Conifers planted round about are of no great age. The high fells, at least, have not changed their appearance much over the years.

A one-way traffic system is in operation on the Tarn road nearest to Coniston. There are car parks and a nature walk.

GRIZEDALE FOREST

(Near Satterthwaite, approached on a steepish road beginning to the south of Hawkshead)

Grizedale Hall was demolished. One of its last duties was to preside over a prison camp for Germans during the 1939-45 war. It was from Grizedale that the only known successful escape of a German prisoner back to his homeland was recorded.

The outbuildings — notably a large stable block — remain and are fully used. Many of the buildings can actually be entered by the public through the courtesy of the Forestry Commission. The stable block is now the Theatre in the Forest, attracting top national talent in a programme of cultural and educational worth. Films and slides of Lakeland wildlife interest are occasionally projected.

In another building is a wildlife museum, dealing exclusively with the beasts and birds of the forest. Tape-recordings impart information and transmit distinctive sounds, such as the roaring of the famous Furness red stags during the rutting season or crooning of blackcock gathering at their *lek* at dawn in spring.

Every facility is granted to visitors interested in wildlife, though expeditions into the forest must be made on foot. There are several recommended walks, including the Silurian Way. The only vehicles allowed are those operated by the Forestry Commission, in the general forest routine. "Hides" from which wildlife can be viewed must be booked in advance.

Grizedale has a camping site, plus a shop. Horn and hair from red and roe deer which are culled as part of the normal forest programme are made up into attractive souvenirs by some of the families of the foresters.

A deep knowledge of forest life is not necessary for an appreciation of Grizedale, for here is a diverse nature trail. Information is available locally by which the forest life can be understood.

CONISTON

(On the A593 between Broughton and Ambleside, being also approached from Greenodd, on the A590, and from Hawkshead)

Coniston village stands on Church Beck, a stream that ripples into Coniston Water. This five-mile-long lake lies only half a mile from the village centre. Coniston is also attached to the name of the best known of the local fells, the Old Man (2,633 feet). The summit can be reached after a two-hour walk from the village.

Something of the history of Coniston can be enjoyed at the small Coniston Museum, where exhibits also include items taken from local sites used in prehistory. Naturally there is much about Victorian John Ruskin, the bestknown resident who arrived in the district to settle at Brantwood in 1871. Ruskin was buried at Coniston.

Walk down to the boat landings and, if you feel disposed, hire a rowing boat. Alternatively, the magnificently restored steam yacht "Gondola" operates a summer service on the lake. Then motor down the eastern side of Coniston Water, passing Brantwood, which is owned by the Educational Trust Ltd., where there is.a fine collection of Ruskin's art work, all of superb quality. The building is "open to view" from February until the end of October. The grounds of Brantwood extend to 250 acres, and include a mile of lake shore. Two nature trails have been laid out.

Visitors to Brantwood are able to see Ruskin's boat, the *Jumping Jenny,* which operated from a harbour he devised with enormous zest. The boat is kept in an outbuilding with Ruskin's coach, a brougham.

E.   Ambleside and the Langdales

AMBLESIDE, "the axle at the wheel of beauty", lies in the very heart of Lakeland. The mountains are close at hand — the twin turrets of the Langdale Pikes and the high, craggy mountains of the Borrowdale volcanics. They back up many a view at Ambleside; they loom mightily above the road at Rydal, where a 90 acre lake has a fringe of tall reeds. The bulk of Loughrigg lies to the south.

Rydal Water and Grasmere, two comparatively small lakes, are only half a mile apart. They might be in different worlds because of intervening high ground. A motorist who uses the main road passes through a gloomy stretch of woodland, turns a corner and sees Grasmere with sudden delight. The main road traverses the edge of the village and then seeks out high ground at the much-improved Dunmail Raise.

What a visitor cannot see from the main road are the side valleys, such as that leading up from Ambleside towards Kirkstone Pass. Out of sight are the deeply-etched Langdales, the small lake of Elterwater and the many higher tarns.

The main road through central Lakeland has numerous tarmacadamed tributaries. Each of them is worth following.

AMBLESIDE

(On the A591, four miles north-west of Windermere)

Ambleside has been a holiday town for many years, and the evidence of this lies everywhere. Yet Ambleside does not cater brashly for the tens of thousands of visitors, who are mainly seeking the older, relatively unspoilt Lakeland. Walk from the town in any direction and the signs of modernity are left behind. There is non-stop variety in the life which goes on at the farms, and many a visitor has had an enjoyable afternoon watching the seasonal routines, such as sheep-clipping and hay-making.

A holiday resort should not be a dormitory for visitors, however fine is the countryside in which it is set. Naturally, those who visit Ambleside have the mountains, lakes and tarns in mind. They want to find out a little more about history and traditions in the Lake District. The Lake District Heritage Centre in Lake Road tells the story of man's effect on the environment over a period of 5,000 years through displays, exhibits, photographs and video films.

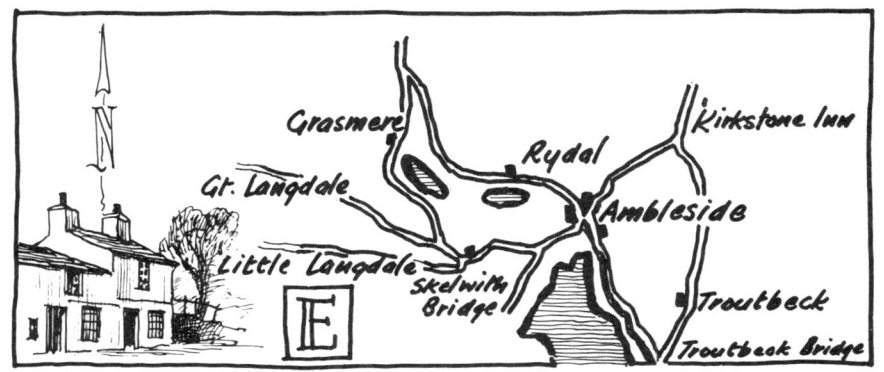

There are times when a visitor is content to potter around the town. Ambleside is an attractive town, with streets at various levels because of the steady downhill development from the original settlement by Stock Ghyll.

Ambleside shops reflect the national trends in marketing, but there are also many goods with a purely local flavour. Lakeland craftsmanship has filled them with objects of utility and beauty — objects made from Lakeland stone, pottery of various kinds, woodwork and art. There are goods which meet the specialist needs of the modern countrygoer, including weatherproof clothing, climbing and skiing equipment.

TROUTBECK

(On an unclassified road which runs parallel to and immediately to the west of the A529 Windermere-Kirkstone Pass road. When approaching from Ambleside turn left past the Low Wood Hotel or at Troutbeck Bridge)

A traveller can soon be in the Troutbeck valley, between Wansfell (1,581 feet) and Applethwaite Common. The main road climbs steadily to Kirkstone Pass, which leads to Ullswater and Penrith. Kirkstone's summit is over 1,400 feet above sea level.

The Troutbeck valley is attractive and historic. The name has not changed since the 13th century. Something of the old way of life can be appreciated at Town End, the home of the Browne family until 1944. Thirteen generations lived at this white-washed 17th century building, which is the last house in the village. Through the ownership of the National Trust it is well preserved and open to the public.

The east window of Troutbeck church contains some outstanding stained glass. The building was enlarged and its tower rebuilt over two centuries ago; a century before that the medieval chapel had been rebuilt.

A local inn is named the *Mortal Man,* from a sign which Julius Caesar Ibbotson painted in the early part of the last century. The sign has since disappeared. On it the artist had shown a lean man and a fat man. The attendant rhyme was: 'O mortal Man, that liv'est on bread, How comes thy

27

Rydal Water, once described as "a mere raindrop of a lake", averages only 25 feet in depth. It is surrounded by pleasant woodland. *(Tom Parker)*

nose to be so red? Thou silly ass that looks so pale, it is by drinking Sarah Birkett's ale."

Among the interesting features of the *Queen's Head,* which lies beside the main road, is the bar which was devised from the frame of a four-poster bed. Shepherds' Meets are held at this inn when stray sheep from the fells are brought together for identification and collection. The informal meeting usually ends with singing and story-telling.

RYDAL

(On the A591 two miles north-west of Ambleside)

Motorist visitors to Rydal are not encouraged to park at the roadside, for this is the busy A591. There are capacious parks at White Moss Common, near the head of Rydal Water, and they are unusual because of their pleasant well-wooded setting. Timber provides variety in colour and shape, and further interest is derived from the Rothay which flows across this low ground.

Dorothy Wordsworth described White Moss Common as "the Alps in miniature". From here a visitor can walk down the farm side of Rydal Water

The Britannia Inn, Elterwater. This Great Langdale village lies at the heart of some of the finest scenery in Lakeland. *(William F. Meadows)*

on Loughrigg Terrace. From the end of the Terrace it is a short step to the Rothay, here crossed by a wooden bridge which gives access to the main road. The final stage of the walk is pleasanter now that the busy road has a kerb.

Rydal Water, smallest of the "great Lakes" (someone described it as "a mere raindrop of a lake"), has a maximum depth of 60 feet but averages only 25 feet. Salmon pass through the lake on their way from the sea to spawning grounds beyond Grasmere.

Rydal Mount, the home of William Wordsworth for 37 years, was purchased by the Wordsworth Trust in 1970 and opened to the public. It still contains many objects known to the poet.

Dora's Field (named after a daughter of Wordsworth), is entered from near the church. Go there in April to see the massed daffodils and narcissi.

GRASMERE

(Just off the A591, three miles north-west of Ambleside)

Grasmere would be an attractive and popular tourist area without its Wordsworthian associations. It lies in a pleasant green vale, almost ringed by mountains. Its river, the Rothay, is joined by a beck from Easedale before flowing into a mile-long lake. The most shapely of the local peaks, which is best seen with the still lake in the fore-ground, is Helm Crag.

Grasmere's strong links with the Wordsworths, William and Dorothy, mean that it enjoys a remarkable popularity. Thousands of tourists annually tramp through the churchyard to inspect the grave of William. About 50,000 people a year visit Dove Cottage, his first Grasmere home, and the nearby museum.

The appearance of Dove Cottage is as near to that of Wordsworth's time as modern man can devise. Even the poet's old clock ticks behind the rough white walls and diamond-paned windows. The adjacent Grasmere and Wordsworth Museum, opened in 1981, sets out William's life story with many personal relics.

A visitor to the Grasmere area who enjoys walking is spoilt for choice. A sense of remoteness will be found in Easedale ("a vale within a vale"), and a track leaves the valley for Easedale Tarn, which is 2½ miles from Grasmere. On the way one can stand to admire a spectacular and long waterfall called Sour Milk Force. Near the tarn is a massive stone forming part of a roofless stone hut near the water.

A highlight of the Lakeland calendar is Grasmere Sports, with its guide races and wrestling in the Cumberland and Westmorland styles. The Sports are attended by over 15,000 people.

GREAT LANGDALE

(Follow the A593 Ambleside-Coniston road to Skelwith Bridge, where fork left on to the B5343. This traverses the length of the valley)

Skelwith Bridge, named after the two-arched bridge crossing the Brathay, has a tourist attraction in Skelwith Force, where the river pours over a 20-foot deep ledge. A riverside path leads to the waterfall.

Further west a motorist peers between trees and sees Elterwater, which means "swan lake" (from the Norse "eltra"). This is really a series of lakes which are shallow enough to interest whooper swans from the far north. The large white birds regularly winter in the Lake District.

The village of Elterwater is viewed across common land. There is much woodland in this area. Charcoal was produced for the production of gunpowder, but the industry had closed down before the last war.

Now the Langdale Pikes are beckoning. By avoiding a left turn for Elterwater, the motorist reaches Chapel Stile, its parish a remarkable 20 square miles. The main place of worship, Holy Trinity Church, celebrated its centenary in 1958, but it replaced a smaller structure (a chapel which was itself rebuilt in 1751).

The Langdale Pikes group together well and are usually thought of by visitors as a single feature. Their names are Harrison Stickle and Pike o' Stickle. A third local highspot is Loft Crag. Antiquarians visit this area because here, four thousand years ago, Stone Age men used a particularly hard rock for axes which were roughly fashioned on the heights of Pike o' Stickle and then finished off in the valleys. These early souvenirs of the Lake District were exported to all parts of Britain.

LITTLE LANGDALE

(Follow the A591 Ambleside-Coniston road and turn right at a point one mile beyond Skelwith Bridge)

Little Langdale is less frequented than its larger neighbour, but here there is the beauty of a tarn, flower-studded fields and fells which include the noble

Wetherlam. Anglicans meet at a chapel-of-ease which is part of a block consisting of four units — church, school, teacher's home and a cottage. Quarrying was once an important industry.

Between the village of Little Langdale and Elterwater lies Colwith Bridge and a waterfall which is worthy of being visited. A small charge is made for admission. Colwith is actually a series of falls, the combined drop of water being about 90 feet.

A post office in Little Langdale was formerly an inn, named *Birch House*. There is a reminder of those days in an iron ring beside the front door, patrons of the inn using it to secure their horses. *Three Shires Inn* was built in 1872, and the deeds mention a "beer house and guest house".

The highest farm in the dale is Fell Foot which has a slated porch on stilts. The Fleming family possessed the farm for many years, acquiring it in 1707. It is now owned, along with much else in the valley, by the National Trust.

Nearby, a road leads across the grain of the country to the head of Great Langdale, and has something of the character of a seaside Big Dipper. A farm near Blea Tarn was known to William Wordsworth, who made it the home of his "Solitary". Wordsworth noted that it was "one bare dwelling, one abode, no more".

The westward exit from the dale is Wrynose Pass, on the line of the Roman road to Ravenglass. It is a long reasonably straight drag with a gradient of 1 in 4. Its name is said to mean "pass of the stallion", the implication being that a strong horse was needed to surmount it. The army used it for tank-training in the second world war.

BLEA TARN FARM

31

F.   Penrith and Ullswater

THIS is the north eastern region of the Lake District, containing Ullswater, a host of quiet little valleys, three sparkling rivers, Pettril, Eden and Eamont (the latter being joined by the Lowther), and some impressive fells.

Penrith itself is situated on low country, but there are great blocks of fells round about. It has always been a pleasant town, and is now by-passed by the M6. Many weary motorway travellers make a break at Penrith for refreshment and to exercise their cramped legs.

Other travellers, visiting the area through choice, motor westwards to Ullswater which, seven-and-a-half miles long and averaging three-quarters of a mile wide, is the second largest stretch of water in the Lake District.

PENRITH

(At a crossing point of major east-west roads and adjacent to the new M6)

Penrith has little industry of the conventional type. Here are few smoking chimneys and expressionless workshops. The prosperity of Penrith is rooted, as it has been for centuries, on the needs of a large and prosperous rural area. It has many shops and services.

The most conspicuous local landmark for travellers is Penrith Beacon, which can be seen on a wooded hill when a motorist is yet some way from town. The stone Beacon is 250 years old.

Robert Adams designed two local houses which, collectively, now form the local Town Hall. The church is large and graceful, Georgian in style. It seems to be a relative newcomer when the crosses and hogsback stones of 10th century date, and standing in the churchyard, are considered.

Penrith castle has been ruined for four centuries but is worth inspecting. At Penrith castle, in the old days, lived Richard, Duke of Gloucester. He built himself a 50 feet long banqueting hall.

LOWTHER WILDLIFE PARK

(At Hackthorpe, four miles south of Penrith on the A6; signposted from junctions 39 and 40 off the M6 motorway)

At the Lowther Wildlife Adventure Park a visitor can drive or walk about parkland abounding in animal and bird life. Close views can be obtained of the many species.

In the Park are deer, including a herd of outstanding Lowther reds which have been in this area for centuries. Comparatively new attractions are enclosures containing European animals and birds, including badger, fox, wild cat, snow and eagle owls. At the badger enclosure one can view badger chambers through glass panels. Visitors can thus see these charming mammals when they are asleep in their "sett".

Many species of waterfowl can be seen. There is a woodland walk that has been stocked with species of tropical birds. Extra seating has been installed beside the woodland walk and around the wildfowl pond. Flamingoes strut in this area.

Naturalness is the general theme. The general impression is of verdant and spacious parkland populated by species of deer, rare cattle and sheep, and even Cheviot wild goats. Facilities for visitors include a large cafeteria and, for the children, what is claimed to be one of the finest adventure playgrounds in Europe.

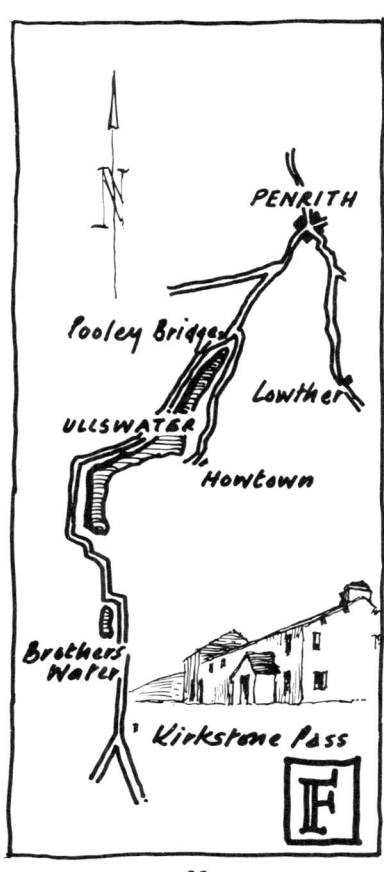

POOLEY BRIDGE AND ULLSWATER

(On the A592 south-west of Penrith)

Pooley Bridge, where Ullswater outflows as the Eamont (a tributary of the Eden) was formerly named Poolhow "the hill by the stream". Ullswater is believed to be named after Ulf, the first baron of Greystoke. It has usually been a quiet, serene lake, an exception being when the Duke of Portland mounted six brass cannon on a pleasure barge and fired them near the rock faces to rouse the echoes!

Travellers on the A592, between Penrith and Ullswater, see the stately Georgian front of Dalemain, for 300 years the home of the Hasell family. Dalemain is open to view at prescribed times. Its ancient core is a pele tower, on to which was grafted a medieval hall and a manor house. The additions culminated in the fine early Georgian extension. The entrance hall is decked with the heads of red deer stalked on 30,000-acre Martindale forest, which is still a part of the estate and still carries red deer. The old banqueting hall has become a tea room; there is a craft shop, and picnic areas have been established in the spacious park. Here, too, is a herd of fallow deer.

One of the curious creatures of Ullswater is the skelly, a sort of freshwater herring. It was feared that the fish had been killed off by pollution from the Glenridding mine (now closed), but the skelly survives. It is most commonly seen near a promontory known as Skelly Nab, southwards from Pooley Bridge. Normally a deep-water fish, the skelly comes into shallow water to spawn in January and February.

Operating on Ullswater, between Glenridding and Pooley Bridge, are the diesel craft *Raven,* which was launched in May, 1889, and the *Lady of the Lake.*

HOWTOWN

(East of Ullswater and located approximtely half way down the shore of the lake)

A narrow, winding road leaves the A592 at Pooley Bridge and extends east of Ullswater. From the road are glimpses of the lake. The best views are obtained from the shores of Howtown Bay. Here, incidentally, are large and colourful buoys connected with water ski-ing. The road has been known to flood near Howtown pier — one of the calling places of the lake motor vessels.

Beyond Howtown are the zig-zags of a steep hill road, the Hause, leading over into the Martindale area. The road should present no difficulties to the careful driver of a modern car. From the head of the Hause, in clear weather, an attractive reach of Ullswater is seen.

The modern Martindale church has an appeal, but even more impressive to students of vernacular architecture is Martindale old church, part way up the valley.

The little roads fanning out from the top of the Hause are all cul-de-sacs.

Ullswater, second largest of the lakes, is nearly eight miles long. This view looks north-east from the head of the lake. *(G. V. Berry)*

That to the right dips down to the small settlement of Sandwick, a name meaning "the sandy creek". Another extends to Dalehead, where an old farmhouse stands.

Martindale, beyond, is the only deer-stalking forest in England. About 250 red deer range generally between Ullswater and Haweswater. Martindale was presumably named from a rare mammal, the pine marten, which is not found in this area today.

GLENRIDDING AND PATTERDALE

(On the A592 at the head of Ullswater and extending to Kirkstone Pass)

Glenridding was formerly a prosperous mining community. Here are many shops and cafés. The pier of the lake "steamer" service is the most conspicuous object by the lake.

Glenridding valley, and neighbouring Grisedale, are approaches to Helvellyn (3,118 feet), the final approach being along the formidable Striding Edge. This ridge appears to be like a razor's edge from a distance.

Winter visitors to the head of Glenridding valley, where the old mine is closed and the area is being tidied up, are skiers. When they have left their cars they still have a good walk to the ski slopes of Raise and Dodds.

Patterdale church is dedicated to St. Patrick, who by tradition passed this way and caused a church to be built. Patterdale's present church was opened in 1858. Within it is a tapestry worked by the late Miss Anne Macbeth.

The name Brotherswater, for a shallow lake seen near Hartsop, is explained as being from a tragedy, in which two brothers died. Extending from near Brotherswater, on a cul-de-sac for cars (though there is a comparatively new car park at the end) is the village of Hartsop. Its architecture is delightfully typical of a small settlement of the Lake District. Some people use the footpath beyond as an approach to the High Street range via Hayeswater.

KIRKSTONE PASS

(Where the A592 reaches a height above sea level of 1,476 feet)

Kirkstone is not the highest pass in Lakeland. It actually lies 13th in the list. This is undoubtedly the highest point a motorist can reach. The road over Kirkstone is not some tiny rural road, but one with an "A" classification. It reaches a height above sea level of 1,476 feet. If you cross Kirkstone you will climb for about 1,000 feet and descend for a similar distance on the other side.

On the summit reaches of the pass stands an inn, *The Travellers' Rest*. Close by, another high road joins the A592. It is a minor road from Ambleside, known — very appropriately — as The Struggle.

The name Kirkstone has been explained as being derived from a large stone beside the pass. Wordsworth wrote: "This block — and you whose church-like frame/Gives to this savage pass its name." De Quincey referred to "this massive church".

From the point of view of a modern car, Kirkstone is not much of an obstacle. Care is needed on a road with innumerable bends and it is wise to use a low gear while descending.

G.

Keswick and Northern Lakeland

THE countryside to the south of Keswick is so spectacular that many visitors do not feel inclined to explore the area to the north. They miss a great deal. There is a vastly-improved road extending west of Bassenthwaite Lake to Cockermouth, where a visit might be paid to the house in which Wordsworth was born. "Back o' Skiddaw" lies Caldbeck, where John Peel the huntsman was born.

From high ground to the north of Caldbeck a motorist can park a car beside a good road and, in clear conditions, look northwards to enjoy one of the fairest panoramas in Britain — of the Cumberland plain, Solway Firth and the blue hills of southern Scotland.

Adjacent to Skiddaw is Saddleback (to use a modern name, the old title being Blencathra). From Threlkeld village, a road heads southwards through the Vale of St. John to Thirlmere.

Keswick became somewhat quieter than it had been with the opening of a new road, which to the east of the town is borne by an immense bridge.

KESWICK

(Capital of northern Lakeland, at a crossing point of the A66 and the A591. A by-pass now takes the A66 clear of the town centre)

Dominating the main street of Keswick is the Moot Hall, now an Information Centre. The building dates back to 1571. When there was a period of rebuilding in 1813 material from Lord's Island on Derwentwater was used. Notice that the Moot Hall clock has only one arm.

For a real sense of history, go to Crosthwaite church, whose story began 1,400 years ago when St. Kentigern journeyed from Carlisle to preach on this spot. Later a cross was erected — hence Crosthwaite. Alice de Romille rebuilt the church in the 12th century, and Sir Gilbert Scott directed the restoration work in 1844. Inside is a white marble effigy of Southey, who lived at Great Hall and is buried in the churchyard.

Keswick's Fitz Park museum (for which there is a small admission charge) includes among its exhibits a rock harmonica played before Queen Victoria. There are geological specimens, local antiquities and a corner devoted to the manuscripts of Hugh Walpole, author of the *Herries* novels. Fitz Park contains a great variety of tree species.

The most prominent landmark in Keswick itself is the spire of St. John's church. In the yard was buried Hugh Walpole. From the yard is an extensive view of Derwentwater.

The large pencil factory at Keswick developed from the discovery of rich deposits of graphite in upper Borrowdale during the reign of Queen Elizabeth I.

Canon Rawnsley, a founder of the National Trust (during the time he was vicar of Crosthwaite) joined with his wife in establishing the School of Industrial Arts, the first object being to secure employment for local men who were left short of work at the end of the tourist season. The enterprise continues to flourish.

BASSENTHWAITE LAKE

(North-west of Keswick, flanked by the A66 and the A591)

A large but comparatively shallow lake, between Thornthwaite Forest and old Skiddaw, Bassenthwaite Lake has been claimed to be the only "lake" in

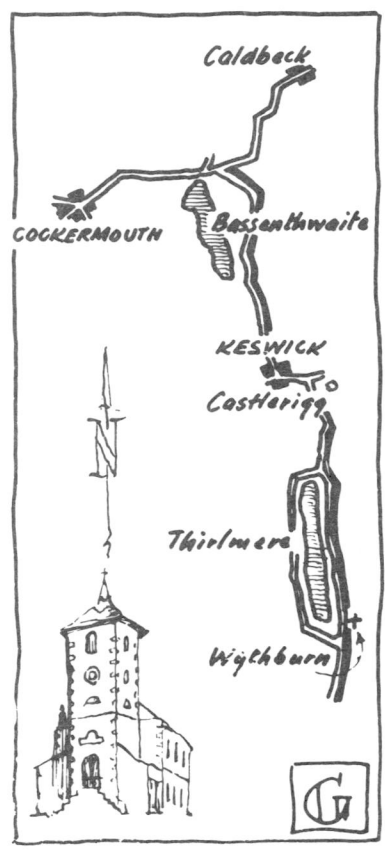

the district, the others having "mere" or "water" in their titles! This district is just outside the main range of fells; the weather can be fine here when rain is descending at Keswick!

On a fell called Barf are fan-like screes up which, many years ago, a man attempted to ride a horse for a wager. He was half way up, and beyond the worst stretch, when horse and rider fell and were killed. Clearly visible from the main road is a commemorative stone. It is annually whitewashed by the landlord of the *Swan Hotel.*

A mile to the south of the *Swan Hotel* is the village of Thornthwaite, home of Thornthwaite Galleries where you will find on sale some of the best paintings, pottery, fabrics and general craft to be found in the north of England. The Galleries contain a coffee-shop which serves home-made lunches.

Bassenthwaite Lake is a centre for dinghy sailing, the bottom end of the lake being leased to a sailing club. The motor journey around the lake involves 18 miles of travel.

CASTLERIGG
(Two miles from Keswick lying a little way off the A591)

Travel either eastwards or southwards from Keswick by the A class roads and you will shortly see signposts indicating Castlerigg, where a stone circle stands. The circle is often called Druid's Circle. There is no evidence to confirm that name.

Here is a ring of 38 stones which were reputedly put in place by men of the Bronze Age 3,000 years ago. Not only is Castlerigg away from the bustle of the main roads, being approached along narrow, winding roads, but it is a superb vantage-point from which to see a great circle of fells.

THIRLMERE
(Is passed on its eastern shore by the A591, to the south of Keswick)

The pressure of traffic on the main road does not encourage loitering here. Two possibilities suggest themselves for those who wish to take a long view of Thirlmere. One is to leave the main road and motor along a smaller road following the western shoreline. The other is to seek out a car park at the point where the A591 is leaving the vicinity of Thirlmere on its way to Keswick. There is a knoll from which visitors can survey the reservoir and the fells round about, and several nature trails have been opened.

Thirlmere was a small lake of 330 acres. Now it is almost four miles long since Manchester Corporation moved in. On 2,100 acres round about have been planted thousands of trees, mainly conifers — Norway and Sitka spruce, Douglas fir, European and Japanese larch, Scots and mountain pines.

Explore Wythburn church, on the eastern side of Thirlmere, close to the point where a footpath leads to the summit of Helvellyn. Wythburn church was high above water level and therefore escaped demolition by the reservoir builders. The church's white walls contrast vividly with the greens and browns of the conifers round about.

The Vale of St. John (a picturesque alternative to the direct route to Keswick from Thirlmere) is four miles long and its stream is the surplus water from Thirlmere, joining the Greta at Threlkeld.

The great mass of Blencathra dominates the Vale. Naddle Fell looms above the valley to the west, and in the east are the northern rocks of the Helvellyn range.

CALDBECK
(On the B5299, back o' Skiddaw)

Back o' Skiddaw the range is far less impressive than when it is seen from Keswick. There are compensations — vast tracts of grassy country, echoing with bird calls, grazed by hardy horned sheep. The sheep's ancestors, in the days when John Peel the huntsman lived hereabouts, provided the mills of Caldbeck with wool they could turn into blankets. Interestingly, this rough blanketing was undyed and known as "hodden grey". Peel, the most celebrated huntsman in the world, wore a coat so "grey", not "gay", as is often written in song books.

John Peel was born about 1776. The ballad about him was composed by his good friend, John Woodcock Graves, one snowy evening in 1829 when "John Peel and I sat in a snug parlour at Caldbeck among the Cumbrian mountains".

What you find "back o' Skiddaw" is a string of little settlements, including Ruthwaite, Uldale, Caldbeck and Hesket Newmarket. John Peel spent his latter days at Ruthwaite (his cottage still stands) but he was buried in Caldbeck churchyard, as you can see if you explore it.

The Caldbeck of the early 19th century had 13 public houses, seven of which survived to within living memory! Now the only inn is the *Rising Sun* (renamed *The Oddfellows Arms*) and the building in which the ballad *D'ye ken John Peel?* was first sung in public.

COCKERMOUTH
(Reached from Bassenthwaite Lake along the A66)

The ruins of a castle dominate Cockermouth, a town which was prospering as far back as the 13th century. Cockermouth was the birthplace of William Wordsworth.

About 5,000 visitors annually tour several of the elegant rooms of Wordsworth's house that are "open to view". Visitors also walk around the garden at the rear — a garden terminating with a riverside walk which Wordsworth was fond of recalling in later years. The house has been owned by the National Trust since 1939.

Among the objects on view is a bureau-bookcase owned by Wordsworth, an inkwell known to the poet, a clock which stood in Rydal Mount during Wordsworth's tenancy and a number of interesting documents and pictures.

Wordsworth House was built in 1745 for John Lucock, Sheriff of Cumberland. It was occupied by John Wordsworth, William's father, when he was agent for the Lonsdales.

Skiddaw from Keswick. "Back o' Skiddaw" lies Caldbeck where John Peel the huntsman was born. *(A. S. Marshall)*

41

H.   Borrowdale and Buttermere

BORROWDALE, Buttermere and Newlands valley are historically linked together by being part of the old Keswick Round. In Victorian times coaches drawn by horses took visitors on an adventurous circuit. The roads were rough and "slippers" — wedgeshaped pieces of wood — were placed under coach wheels for braking, on steep descents.

The main road through Borrowdale and up Honister Pass is followed by the majority of visitors. Some venture on a winding way from near Derwentwater to Watendlath. Others seek out Seathwaite, at the dale head, reputedly the wettest place in England. Its annual average rainfall is over 120 inches. Cars may be parked at the roadside near the famous farm.

Honister leads over to Buttermere, a lake with some majestic pines at its head. The shadows from high hills extend far across the valley.

DERWENTWATER

(Lying to the south of Keswick, edged to the east by the road to Borrowdale)

Derwentwater has been called the Queen of the English Lakes. It looks most regal in autumn, when there are massed trees showing a range of tints and multi-tinted leaves float on still water.

In shape, Derwentwater is an oval. The length is about three miles, and the width about half that distance. It is well viewed from Friars Crag, near the boat landings, which is also a vantage point for the Borrowdale Fells.

Derwentwater has several islets, including Derwent, Lord's, St. Herbert's and (a curiosity) a floating island which occurs spasmodically near the Lodor boat landing. The temporary island is supposed to be brought up by methane created by decaying reeds on the lake bed.

The Keswick and Derwentwater Launch Company, formed in 1933, is responsible for providing boating facilities on Derwentwater. The journey round the lake takes about 50 minutes. Excellent times for viewing the lake and its environs are June and September.

Derwentwater has a vast catchment area. The difference between low and high water is about nine feet. The water level rose 6 feet 8 inches in 24 hours during the August Bank Holiday of 1938!

EAST OF DERWENTWATER

(Features beside the Keswick-Grange road)

Details of local interest can be obtained from an attractive information centre set up close to the boat landings by the National Trust. From the

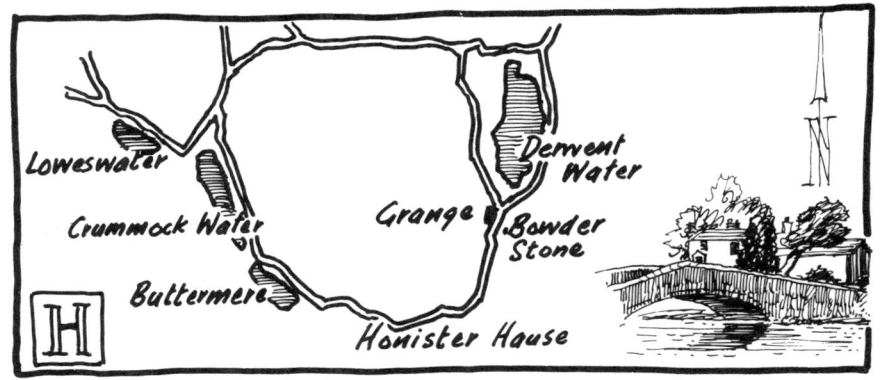

centre can be seen Brandelhow, at the other side of the lake. This was the first property to be owned in the Lake District by the National Trust, one of the pioneers of which was Canon Rawnsley, then vicar of Crosthwaite.

A road extending from near the lake shore to Watendlath climbs a hill to Ashness Bridge. Later there is a "surprise view" of Derwentwater. Watendlath has a small tarn, and a footpath leads beside it and then over to Borrowdale. The Watendlath road, a cul-de-sac, is not recommended to motorists during the main holiday season. The congestion can be terrifying.

Barrow House, near the south-eastern shore of Derwentwater, one of Lakeland's largest youth hostels (80 beds), was originally known as Cascade Hall. Hostellers in the dining room can look out on Barrow Falls — 108 feet, in two falls — which are the second highest falls in the Lake District, first place in the list being occupied by Scale Force, Buttermere.

GRANGE AND THE BOWDER STONE

(Where the Derwent flows into the lake)

Grange is approached over bridges spanning the Derwent. The river water is clear and looks green, the green shade coming from the fragments of slate in the bed. The slate was washed down over many years from quarries high up the valley.

Anyone who motors through Grange takes the road high above the western shore of Derwentwater, leading back to Keswick, and passes near Brakenburn. This was the home of Hugh Walpole, author of the *Herries Chronicle*. Grange was often mentioned in print by Walpole.

There is a craft centre by the Borrowdale road near Grange. In an area of birches stands the immense Bowder Stone. A ladder reared against it enables people to climb on to the stone, which is 36 feet high and has been estimated to weigh 1,970 tons.

Ashness Bridge on the road to Watendlath, providing one of the most renowned viewpoints in the Lake District with distant Derwentwater and the Skiddaw range.

HONISTER PASS

(Link between Borrowdale and Buttermere, starting near Seatoller)

From Seatoller the road climbs steeply for about a mile, and at the summit a traveller is nearly 1,200 feet above sea level, shadowed by the lofty north face of Fleethwith Pike.

The Buttermere and Westmorland Green Slate Company operates quarries around the top of Honister. In recent years a new quarry has been opened out at 1,860 feet above sea level, but this quarry is not visible from the main road.

Slate-quarrying is one of the traditional industries of Lakeland, and at Honister there is work for over 30 craftsmen. The main effort is in the preparation of the attractive olive-green slates which are sent all over Britain and are being used increasingly as roofing material. Flooring tiles are produced, many for export.

BUTTERMERE

(Traversed by the B5289, between Honister and Lortonvale)

Buttermere and Crummock Water occupy the same valley in what many visitors must consider to be the most spectacular area of Lakeland. There are steep-sided fells to tempt walkers, connecting farms and the small village of Buttermere. Across the lake is Scale Force, with a single leap of 120 feet, adding to the grandeur of the scene.

Gatesgarth, at the Buttermere side of Honister Pass, is a typical fell farm, with 2,700 acres of ground, some of it "inland" (valley ground fenced round), but mostly consisting of wild, rough fell on which about 2,500 sheep, mainly of the Herdwick breed, are found. The farmers of the Buttermere valley maintain a loyalty to the traditional Herdwick breed as being best suited to the local conditions. You will also see beef cattle, known locally as sucklers.

Hassness, just north of Buttermere, is a house run by the Ramblers' Association. The itineraries planned for outings from Hassness give some idea of local attractions. On one walk, a lakeside path is followed to Buttermere and Scale Force with continuation alongside Crummock Water to *Kirkstile Inn*, Loweswater, then through Lanthwaite woods to Rannerdale and back to Buttermere.

There is also a ridge walk following an ascent of Whiteless Pike, Grasmoor and Crag Hill. The outing extends along the ridge to Sail, Scar Crags and Causey Pike, returning by Sail Beck.

CRUMMOCK WATER AND LORTON

(A continuation northwards of the Buttermere valley)

A motorist near the two-and-a-half mile long Crummock Water can appreciate elemental Lakeland. There is little of man's work to divert the attention of the natural scene and some of the shapeliest hills in Britain — Mellbreak, Grasmoor, Red Pike, High Stile.

Greylag geese are seen on the lake during the nesting season. There are red squirrels in the area. And in the lake itself are char, fish living in the cold depths but coming into shallow water to spawn. Char have been landlocked here since the Ice Ages.

Lorton valley, between Crummock Water and Cockermouth, sends a high road over Whinlatter to Keswick. By the side of Whinlatter, the Forestry Commission has planted thousands of conifers, which give stretches of the road the flavour of the Canadian backwoods. The Whinlatter Pass Visitor Centre tells the story of the Lakeland forests.

I.   Eastern Lakeland

THE best approach to this region is from the M6. A traveller quickly notices a contrast between high-speed travel on a motorway and low-gear travel on roads that seem to have an aversion to going straight. The motorway driver, travelling north, passes through Lune Gorge, seeing on the right the impressive grouping of the Howgill Fells. He should turn off at Shap, crossing moorland to the old A6.

The eastern fells can be penetrated by a number of small valleys, each of which carries the northern term of "dale".

LONGSLEDDALE

(Approached from the old A6 to the north of Kendal)

The sign by the A6 indicates "Longsleddale 4½ miles". At this distance stands the dale church. The road to it is one of the most winding, constricted roads in Cumbria. Six miles from the main road are the farmsteads of Sadgill, originally a Norse settlement. At eight miles from the A6 the travellers — now on foot — can look into Wren Gill, which is the source of the river Sprint.

Longsleddale does not include the hamlet of Garnett Bridge, though this lies down in the valley. Look out for a farm just beyond the hamlet. It is prominently named Dale End.

The church is the latest of several that have occupied the site. It was built just over a century ago but the oldest piece of church silver is a chalice dated 1571. This is one of the oldest chalices extant in England. A cupboard dated 1661 is of the type made for spice and salt and probably stood in one of the cottages.

Longsleddale is deep, with hills rising to the 2,000 feet contour on both sides of the valley. The old farms were well sited to cheat the weather. Low Sadgill is 670 feet above sea level. The name Sadgill relates to a "saeter by the gill", saeter being Norse for a farm or shieling.

HAWESWATER

(Cul-de-sac from Bampton,. a village close to Shap)

In recent times, Manchester Corporation set a concrete dam in the mouth of old Mardale. A pleasant mere was extended into an all-embracing reservoir.

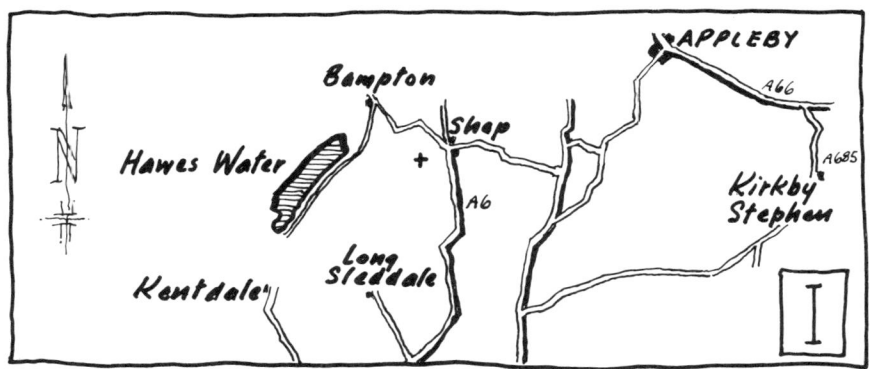

The scenery remains sublime, especially a horseshoe shape of fells at the dalehead.

Bampton church is (like that of Patterdale, eight miles to the west) dedicated to St. Patrick. A pleasant road runs south-westwards to where the dam of the Manchester reservoir is seen, partly shielded by trees. (The dam is actually best seen from a distance, as during the descent to Bampton from Shap.)

The community in Mardale had to leave as the water was impounded. Demolished were the little church and the *Dun Bull Inn,* formerly a wellknown gathering place for fox-hunters and fell-walkers. Crowds flocked to the valley during the drought of 1984 when many of the remains became visible. From the terrace of the *Haweswater Hotel,* about mid-way along the shore of the reservoir, there is an uninterrupted view of the western fells. Red squirrels frolic on the trees behind the hotel.

Hotel patrons are among the limited number of people who are allowed to fish in the lake, its tributaries and the dam in the neighbouring Wet Sleddale. The fish are brown trout and char, the latter staying in the depths, except at spawning time. The old technique of trolling for char is not allowed.

From the car park at the end of the road are several attractive footways, one (by Blea Water) leading up on to High Street (2,663 feet).

SHAP ABBEY

(Lies close to, but out of sight of, Shap village, from which it is signposted)

The ruins of this abbey stand on a three-acre site beside the Lowther and are open to public viewing, being maintained by the Department of the Environment. Shap was founded by Thomas Gospatrick at Preston Patrick early in the 12th century as a convent for Premonstratensian canons. It was moved to Shap later in the century.

The most impressive feature of the remaining masonry is the west tower, which dates from the 16th century. The custodian uses wooden spatulas (as did the monks) to remove moss from the rather flaky stone of the ruins. He has to trim and weed around the two miles of edges where the lawns are adjacent to the stonework.

SHAP ABBEY